music for landing planes by

music

for

landing planes

by

éireann lorsung

MILKWEED EDITIONS

Published 2007 by Milkweed Editions
Printed in Canada
Cover design by Percolator
Cover and interior art, "Plenty," by Jennifer Davis
Interior design by Percolator
The text of this book is set in Mrs. Eaves.
07 08 09 10 11 5 4 3 2 1
First Edition

Special funding for this book was provided by the Jerome Foundation.

Milkweed Editions, a nonprofit publisher, gratefully acknowledges sustaining support from Emilie
and Henry Buchwald; the Bush Foundation; the Patrick and Aimee Butler Family Foundation; CarVal
Investors; the Timothy and Tara Clark Family Charitable Fund; the Dougherty Family Foundation;
the Ecolab Foundation; the General Mills Foundation; the Claire Giannini Fund; John and Joanne
Gordon; William and Jeanne Grandy; the Jerome Foundation; Dorothy Kaplan Light and Ernest
Light; Constance B. Kunin; Marshall BankFirst Corp.; Sanders and Tasha Marvin; the May Department
Stores Company Foundation; the McKnight Foundation; a grant from the Minnesota State Arts
Board, through an appropriation by the Minnesota State Legislature, a grant from the National
Endowment for the Arts, and private funders; an award from the National Endowment for the Arts,
which believes that a great nation deserves great art; the Navarre Corporation; Debbie Reynolds; the
St. Paul Travelers Foundation; Ellen and Sheldon Sturgis; the Target Foundation; the Gertrude Sexton
Thompson Charitable Trust (George R. A. Johnson, Trustee); the James R. Thorpe Foundation; the Toro
Foundation; Moira and John Turner; United Parcel Service; Joanne and Phil Von Blon; Kathleen and Bill
Wanner; Serene and Christopher Warren; the W. M. Foundation; and the Xcel Energy Foundation.

Library of Congress Cataloging-in-Publication Data

Lorsung, Éireann, 1980–
    Music for landing planes by / Éireann Lorsung.
        p. cm.
    ISBN-13: 978-1-57131-428-4 (pbk. : acid-free paper)
    ISBN-10: 1-57131-428-8 (pbk. : acid-free paper)
    I. Title.
PS3612.O77M87 2007
811'.6—dc22

2006033341

This book is printed on acid-free paper.

NATIONAL
ENDOWMENT
FOR THE ARTS
A great nation
deserves great art.

MINNESOTA
STATE ARTS BOARD

BA ZCLC
MMM MWC SY

+ M D M C N

music for landing planes by

music for landing planes by

It will not come by waiting for it. It will not be a matter of saying "oh, here it is" or "there it is." Rather, the kingdom of God is stretched out upon the earth, and people do not see it.

The Gospel of Thomas

Being

A letter is holy. A story
is holy hands reaching out into the world.
Birds come home
          across distance I can't conceive

and live in their bodies.
Ash in the air. Every place I've been
is on fire with words.

     One day
I throw away all my love letters
without noticing. Mountains

in the heart.
          What belongs
to me? I leave the world
all the time. These arms, these

fingers, this tongue, these feet,
and their bent wings. I know
it will be dirt, the prayers

now in marrow will retake
earth. I will live inside whatever flies.
Burning, the brink of all things.

Bedtime

Capucapu is the noise my heart makes when I am falling asleep.
My hands are quick and silent monkeys, their proper ermine ruffs.

Ushers in carmine warn us not to make a peep.
And everything is hush and falling snow,
purple the snow makes sky, the way a streetlight glows.

Nighttime's playbook opens page by page.
The velvet room can spy each trick of air.

Nighttime stands before me, my heart, my lively hands.
She inks the city sleeping into spots of light.
What she wants us to believe is what we can't believe is there.

My heart sings to my palms: *capucapu.*
This speckled night is freezing every breath.

Together in the quiet, hands and monkeys keep an earnest watch.
A clock is singing somewhere in the dark.
And nighttime's strength is wasting in the early breaking arc.

When I Was Crossing a Prairie

Once the ragweed came up dense and haunted
us in the night. I couldn't sleep
for the feathers and the breathing
tubes. The Volvo sped the hill, I remember
oxygen. Snails crept in

their shells faster than air. The livelong
day you sang, happily stapling
your thumb to the desk. I hated you
for turning the sandbox dirty,
finding cat poop under the swings. In the violets
behind the house you buried
every animal I tried to own. Now I am so

much older. Look, I'm leaving, but
still pushing the green hose through sand
volcano rivers and moats, break and float
stick bridges. I remember
toybox with the tiny clowns and knock
on my wall, the dark leaving
me somewhere behind and my eardrum
falling from my ear with a tiny click
to the floor of the number
22 bus, heading downtown.

Things I Want to Say

Your brother lost his virginity at seventeen. The dark
upstairs, your parents asleep in one room:
he was there, where passing cars made movies out of light

and his walls—alone with a girl, some girl, who knows
which girl it was.

I know you were in the same house, another girl, two years older,
same late kind of night. All confidences in the nightlight's circle.

I don't know what it's like to be amazed and seventeen.
One night, I want to be each pair of lips
that presses against ankle, elbow. Two kids
standing up, awkward, her hair messy.

I want to lie next to you
when you are nineteen and there,

in that specific dark, I want to be the girl who willingly offers
her body to another person.

For years I waited near walls
or on chairs with my ankles crossed, white gloved,

pastel. Everyone waited for the same thing: that other
hand, those lights on strings near the ceiling.

In high school the roof was high as heaven,
Christian Brothers chaperoning each swaying pair.
Sex was something we made jokes about. I had a dirty mouth.

I held on to the boy
in front of me for show or out of loneliness, I hoped

he didn't have b.o. when I laid my cheek on his shoulder,
I counted out my future children's names like stars,
I let him touch my back
under my shirt.
I was waiting for something.

You chaste women, you teaching Brothers, tell me:
Is it this, silence like mourning between two people?

Doing

I am filling the pot with water to boil. My mother's feet
are swollen as sausages.
They curl, and her fingers curl, and they don't release.
Her back is full of arthritic fire.

She is the cold one, now; I give up heat to her.
Every night, my brothers ignore her limp
upstairs. She would rather be ignored.

I want to pour the water over my hands, want
them to blister red and white. I want
to forget.

In the Chinese restaurant six years ago
I tilted a pot of tea over the edge of a table, caught
pot and water together in one palm.
This is it, an anointing: heat
becoming balm.

I want my mother
taking care of me. Not her back sliced in half, her hands
crabbed like an old woman's, not psoriasis,
not tumors, not hair falling out all over the house.

Before I knew what death
was like, I would cut my stomach in even lines.
Sometimes I see the razor's stern edge parting my skin
but I can't lift it, can't make the imagined a verb.
I can't pretend it's something distant

anymore, some glamorous thing to die
like girls in movies. I know what it is:

six prescriptions. The insurance company's warning.
My father holding my mother's hand
where the cracks run deep and bleed of their own accord.

The World and the Ocean and the Sky

I hope you lose your mother tongue complete
the bitter line around your mouth. Girl standing
on a fire hydrant. Amen, someday you will break

every bone in your body, your pelvis will shatter
the iron rod, water pressure. The six-inch bolt
and the thin line of blood.

Is there any among us who could forget baleen?
Deep the water outside: sinks narwhal, one horn
spiraling night- and daytime, explorer's waking

dream. And early for funeral blacks. It is not
the man; it is a wax cast of him. The bodies
straps of leather at the earth's mouth, pulleys

singing Miserere nobis. You come like deer
to water. All summer was a knife's honed
edge on wrist skin, a reed broken. This is the voice
calling to you in the wilderness.

How My Name Came to America

After some time people want to forget

There are years
between names   they said *take him home to die*
no one could survive   like this

                             and most do

Water from the Catskills. See, here is the eleven-year-old
here is the *Gates of Heaven*   here the bunged leg
the bowler hat   Jersey City   Winfield Park
half sister in the upstairs window
                     then the Bronx
Telly Foster   this house on Parsonage Street [12 dollars/mo]
to New York City   (to Prospect Park)   & meanwhile

     born at the beginning of the end Ellen Dinan in Co. Cork
     Timothy O'Callaghan, place unknown
     and a hammer dropped from an I beam fifty stories up.

Where it is broken   it is unredactable
              there are fingers caught under wheels

In time someone begins to speak the language
proper   *go mbeannaí Dia thú*   like an old man

We were taken from them & remade
into beauty   letters marching calmly down
the throat until naming   [Woman] O'Neill
is forgotten: Bríd to Bridget   [___ McK & wife]

to Delia. To John, Matthew, Thomas,
Henry, Elizabeth, Jeannette:

Eóin, Maitiú, Tomás, Anraí, Eilís, Sinéad

what was lost was lost in planting the land with new crops
              the rock-edge cliffs to the Atlantic—

They send their hunger forward from 1560,
five-pound note in hand
and the one there to meet it watches his father's
    leg catch and flame: gangrene
                        like dawn taking over the sky

And it catches in Tellygarvin, in Annagelliff,
        in Celbridge, Rathcormick, Mallow, Schull
and fathers watch their daughters leave   if they live
to see them   sometimes what is past is living alongside us
    docks in the morning
            —this is a kind of promise *go ndeisí mé*

What if one's life were not a commodity, not something to be bartered to the highest bidder or made to order? What if one's life were governed by needs more fundamental than acceptance or admiration? What if one were simply to stay home and plant some manner of garden?

Paul Gruchow, *Grass Roots: The Universe of Home*

And Will Be

The only thing there is here
    is the word.

Go along road, through tunnel, under bridge

Muscat, lily
        the whole world reduces

I was born before zeroes and ones defined the shape of rivers
before crossing an ocean equaled a bomb in midair
somewhere students kept hostages
somewhere a landslide covered everything in mud
and these were real
        the Word wants to touch

If you need healing,
just go to the doctor, I mean
that familiar spine, and open it. A lion
waits. A field of bobolinks.
The doorways and speckled streets
and blackbirds.
    But this isn't
    information.

(And the Word was)
        They take up *yes* and *no* and do not rest

on a single answer. My students
want everything, both, they urge into the classroom
saying *what if* to their own minds.
One day they all sleep. *Papaver somniferum.* I go
among them to open
a dissection

inside they carry polished stones, the roots
where wings join
                                back, the wind blowing
water white & black

                I want to climb into their wolf bodies
and live there while they relearn
the world, deleting binary.

If they can, I hope
every person in the world will say *yes*
                which is the trumpet flower blooming over a wall

                which is tinged by lack, but rejects that lack:
                                instead, going everywhere, bright red, insistent

Maybe there is no hope
in some darkness. Nothing
any word can approach.

Well, still, sing out
into that darkness. Sound
the shapes of rocks

and shorelines. If your words
don't come back,
keep singing.

(Lucky life is like this—)

Whenever I can I will go out into the world singing.

(Amen, alleluia)

The Way to Really Love It

Touch the edge of salt pond with a finger. Maps
don't show the taste of water.
                              You can know

what cows eat by tang in butter, and here
what swims, what stays away

tells saltiness. If you wade
hip deep in these ponds, maybe
                              something will begin

or something will stop happening.
Places like this

are dying off. Between land & ocean,
you stop thinking of it and it's gone.
                              Sudden

lack of birds. Pitch pine. A bog quaking
to life, with life, you had better

listen to this disappearing land, you had better
be quick, keep it trimmed,
                              burning—

Bird Woman, Duck Hunting

What is the first miracle she performs?

(Not rescuing the brother in winter.

                            Not the hole in the sky.)

Marshland is full of birds   flight and early

in the morning   dark

heart turns
      to wing & wind

      Shooting across dawn

Holy   holy   holy

      is the name
                & ducks tip from the sky.

She puts on their bodies before teeth and hair can find her

      Long quiet

                            then the guns again

Matins, Standard Time

after Louise Glück

Last night what was hidden in earth
came out of the earth.

I don't tell you these things
so you will worry,
so you will move closer
to the dark tunnel that waits
at the beginning of winter when time
changes. I want to hold
your shoulders as you bend
to inhale the vegetable smell of bulbs
and the spearmint rhizomes.
Here in the open

we don't have to be afraid of the world,
with its hurricanes and its long nights.
Look at the onion plants,
sprouting anew, even though the longest
night is closer now,
even though you had believed they were done
giving out their fragile glory.

Oceanside

Waves or fish in deep water   and light
         on their backs and singing

        out of nowhere the song   waves

        make slapping again   lichen

            covered   the rock floor   it rises

Yes   to sing is something

        even pure animal knows   what comes
                     is fear   unbroken

and so in the black   in the turning moon they break

and break and are singing

Exclusion Pregnancy

Sister, what is growing
in this body? Either it is blood

or it is lack of blood, I hear
around the world women

grow monsters:
sixth fingers, intestine

wrapped around neck, babies
joined at the face, radioactive

treasures. Listen to the empty
fields where slate blows

into dust and everything built
glows at night. You eat

no soft cheese, no pesticide
but your double there in the reactor's

heart, she burns into the same
fullness, she feels a triple

beat, she knows how long
things are for this world

in soft dust she lies down
her children lie down to sleep.

Hail Mary

SNJ

1)
There is blue in the world; for instance, this scarf
from a stall near Rialto.

                   In Venice I never worried

because everyone thought I was Italian. But I walked
with one hand on my bag.

2)
At our parallel, in December, light
dims. To blue. Our star is moving

on the other side. I believe
there is a woman holding the world

like a little girl holds an egg
she finds in the grass in springtime:

blowing warm breath on it.
You can know good will rise

from things, even if you don't live to see.

3)
My sister looks out the window. She will have a baby
when the first flowers are done blooming.

Peonies. She thinks it will be a girl, born (I know it) between dark
and day and blue with air & effort. Girl of the future,

I'm sending you a crown airmail, made of bluebells, hydrangeas,
    hyacinths.

4)
Could you touch the stranger?
Next to you on the bus. Line at the bank.
Don't imagine oceans there, but currents
like electricity.
We stretch out of ourselves
without permission. The body
receives annunciations anytime,
unawares. It is magic,
I can say this, it is not
to be possessed, not willing to be tamed.

5)
If somewhere someone is dying in pain, forgive me.
The world, the ocean, and the sky adore you. Infinite.

You notice everything and you
are reason. The stars go out and we
break each other open. What is it

to be so large you can love us when we are so awful?
Stealing good out of the body's broken pocket.

6)
The pledge is, love everything here. For a little while,
which is all.

Once, there was no place for me. So I lived where I could.
I held on to words, my body,
the lily that was my husband.

Sisters, in this cold world, give out the heat you carry.
        Say yes, as long as you can.

Excavation

Who says the polars are stirring? Ice
on top of the world sleeps longer, deeper
than a man frozen in it. In ages
there may be nothing to search for,
found bone, no excavation. Near Padua

a young man with curly hair brushes dirt
from grave markers with his thumbs
and no one mourns. He cannot feel
the incremental movement of glacier
down the slope. Spring rises even
in March and the air—he wants it healing

as it should. Shreds of cloth
decay an ancient torso and his mind
clears hair. Ossuary, ring holder, sometimes
he falls in love with the Roman girl,
holds her petrified finger in one palm
until darkness crosses the hills.
My dear friend Nicolas will one day be dead

and someone else will find his bones,
love them. If I could see
far ahead, I would want to know which place
will honor us, which museum make
us into marvels, twine gold into our hair
where once was only leaf and vine.

Forgetting in Multiple

There are repairs to be made
in the smell of the underground hallway

      a bird   hologram
      a struck match

So much flickers here
in the chase lead letters sit heavy

& I wait

Something tastes like licorice,
an old man sitting on an old wall near the sea

and sewage waiting
      saturation comes early in the morning

One day it will be July again and I will wake up
in Venice where nothing   apparates correctly

printshop waiting

and my body flickering between the Saints
the razor scraper flying over sheets

      lumberyards
      the dream of salt water

All subterranean, all hushing
aluminum, shadows of blue boats

the year rushing rushing forward to meet me, over and over

Forecast

At this point everything
depends.
     Where I am called,
who is calling, whether

I answer. My hands
are feathers
     on the wing
of a bird tearing itself apart

flying in all the directions.
Which heart
     asks me to come
here, to stay. To rest,

something the wild animal
cannot do.
     I am getting old
in my body, I say.

     If you just
want snow at night
or rain streaming
     over your face,

maybe in ten years I'll fly the long
flight east
      maybe we'll find
one another near the coast

where lights don't dim
in late hours,
      museum where you keep
the past I ignore, storm I can't survive.

Methinks it is a token of healthy and gentle characteristics, when women of high thoughts and accomplishments love to sew; especially as they are never more at home with their own hearts than while so occupied.

Nathaniel Hawthorne, *The Marble Faun*

St. Stephen's Day

AL

All winter long I can hear the cries of birds in the thatch.
They come down from the north to hide

in eaves, wind forgotten, the lake looming out
of memory and their bones beating with blood.

Where is the one who will hold birds in his hands
for me? While on earth I sing and practice Advent.

I look for the face in the rafters. Drifting to me
little pieces of hay, flecks of peat ash promise something:

maybe it is spring.
                    I hold with waiting. I hold with hands
that are larger than mine, spanning the shores

of the Great Lakes. I hold with the white snow pushing back
the sky and the empty hours between houses.

Fill up the rooms with singing alone, I say. Who knows
what will thaw in six months. Make the song

and eat it yourself. Thus live the birds in the thatch, wrens.
If I dream in the smoke-draped room I dream

a little boy to dance under a cape of straw
                                        the hushing
wings built full of air, scuff of a foot at the door.

(I am never afraid to open—)

Dressmaker

Nothing touches like tan velvet touches
the palm. Now the cracks come, because what gives
without taking?—Doesn't exist. Say

you forget what is lanolin, what is raw about fleece
uncarded & unwashed. Say the silver feel
of charmeuse lines your sleep. You've lost

what there was before pins & needles, sound
a scissors makes through cloth on a hardwood floor,
thick waist of the dressmaker's dummy. Don't tell me

any more. Without Burano lace, without cinnabar
strung on a cuff, shantung and satin and netting and swiss:
no rich man, no camel, no needle's threatening eye.

Gnosis

In the beginning, in the full room, by 40-watt light I am stripping
duct tape from a mannequin's body:
paper and cloth. Every time I tear her
I feel pressure in my sinuses like crying
and I apologize out loud. This is an object.
But shouldn't I honor this body
like any body?
                    Someone made the leather cuff
around the shoulder.

Tonight, I don't think while I work.
Maybe three hundred miles west of here a girl my age
is being beaten by her husband
and I won't know until tomorrow. Let me rest.

What right—to rest? The ought to says *throw away*
the toys and *feed my sheep, why are you playing*
with scissors and a broken doll
when my girl lies in Fargo with a fat lip.

I believe in the resurrection and the life of the world to come,
but I want this one.
                    Tell me, why does the man
strike at the heel, soft in flesh as a serpent?
Sometimes night is so long. And, forgetting,
she won't lie alone, but goes to pour milk
and wait for the second shift to end. Halfway
through: there is the unplugged receiver
and the coat that never made it to the squad car.

Where the muslin breaks
it is broken for ever. Fibers stick
to fibers in the tape, cotton
tufts out and dusts the air. I may take
needle to this old body, darn together
or patch with cotton. Or scissors, and lay her bare
and flat, make a new skin.
                    In the morning
she will be there, night rolled away by some angel.

No one waking remembers
what has been put asunder by their hand:
thank you, that I can still trust the body
to press on, not knowing why, just breathing
and beating until dark comes, or sleep, or sense, or light.

Putting the Winter in New Hampshire

What round. When silence bends
into mountain, here in the arc of pure
last lights and stalking trees. And you.

Dark always comes, layers
over snow the color of ash, color
of bone. Your hands touch everything

near you, boards of the weathered house
warping in wet air. Woodpile
a danger in the evening claimed

arm by arm. How your hands do it,
which is to say taking everything in, a gather
of wood and small dogs, stove

and staircase, a hush in the evening
to light the darkened snow.

Volans

the constellation flying fish

What is the meaning of flying fish?
Biplanes in a water-green world.
What more could sound suggest than artless object?
—what to signify with *cattail*? With *milkweed*?

Afternoon.
Succulence for burnt flesh. Rest.

—a flight of birds.
A simple samara, one-winged seed. A silver dollar.

What is the fruit
of the ash?

Be sure what it is you collect:
datura—violent capsule, breeding prickles.

Nothing can question nighttime,
how stars scatter like birds or seeds.

What plan, symmetry?—the carpals
of a netted leaf, a hand, a dorsal?

Except beauty. Except nights
when only fish break the surface.

The quick, plastic scent of belladonna.
The cottonwood leaves murmuring like shoals.
The easy membrane of moon on the water.

The goldfinch, the wren, and the owls;
the kingfisher and the vulture.

Who watches tonight?

What shadow slides from tree to tree,
from leaf to leaf like a rain
of scales? Like a leap, into the air?

If you slip your fingers through the soft musk of thyme,
what scent will cling to your hand?

If your hand, brushing upward, catches a fin in the palm,
what will you believe in the morning?

Lejermål

I want him to walk out of his frame.
Pictures of red-wing birds flying out of hay.

    [The road

        the wheels of grass   the bending
        to touch in daylight his hands full of chaff

When I was little my hands cut from handling straw.
Pleated skirt. White shirts covered the world

        all there was to see from the road   disappeared
        into brush   afternoons without water

This was some sort of love.
        In shadow
(Or was lying.)
        and in shade   and dapple   we would go down

        ourselves thirsting and bind   the alder stumps]
A thousand feet up from ocean, my arms became geese returning

the formation. And now.   I rest.
What I cannot do more. Where I cannot go.

Printmaking

Why don't you print the sky
at eight thirty? I saw your studio: it was filled
with things I didn't put there. Silk
flowers, turpentine in a honey jar,
an alligator's head cut
from its body. *Etch,*
you said. *Intaglio.* On the wall, a copper plate
ad infinitum, each impression
eaten more by acid.

I meander
on my two wheeler, the last cold
of spring slapping me. Measure it
by ink and rollers, measure it in tire
spins—up the pedestrian bridge:
me and Venus, we're hanging in the air.
Look at the ants

on my bathroom tile—their circles
describe the Golden Mean. I spray
acid, hope their bodies curl within a day.
                              Meanwhile,
the press rolls on. Yes, somewhere
people stand in shadows. Yes, somewhere

I am sleeping, and you are bent, applying ink
        to plate. The sky
is still there and brilliant blue, convex.

What I want to ask you I can't ask you, because
when I'm with you we're in this world
where the walls are hung with your
implements and I am dwarfed by teeth
and feathers, wide
circles inscribing into everywhere, Pompeiian columns
rendered flat and huge—

You should have printed this sky. I don't care
whether you use litho or relief, if you're printing (again)
that circle *ex* copper plate, you know
that's what it is, Venus or the moon and their proper places,

me, my bicycle's double hoop,
the curling bodies of ants. *It's all come 'round
to this,* and you grinned
at your own pun. I leave each room
and the room again is perfect.

The One You Love

Sister, you are sitting far across the world
your hands   in your lap   in the window's elegant
crossed shadows.

     I am a giant, I see
both corners of earth
I watch the one you love grow before you know him
and you   rising to your toes in a pleated skirt

to sing. *This is my sister,* this
is a boy born with birds for hands, a sweetened date
for a tongue.
     There are some who will pull the wings
off every thing that flies. So a boy finds himself
in sand, a girl in water, and birds always
in air   I would part
     these elements to bring him
to you, so late   as sweet, as bitter as almonds
after hours in the dry air—

Dreaming of the Printmaker (2)

In the name of the father, in the little brown house
your mother is waiting by the window. Long hair
shining in the light. There is no money

so she catches birds in her hands. She eats
their bones and makes a hat out of their feathers for you
so you will grow up strong. When the loom

says *clakclak* she goes to it, stringing warp
and woof together, pulling
cloth from the air and making rugs. She knows

you will be born late at night in May.
Because she is your mother she is jealous
of the girls who will love you, even before they are born.

—That your hands will be firm and good
at work, the lathe and the hasp. She will raise you
like a falcon raises her young, proud

and always afraid of the shadow coming to nest.
She knows the birds are watching.
You fix the broken piano, her heart.

She picks up the shuttle at the loom
and stripes of cloth outline a maddered boy.

Dressmaker, Shadow

Dresses hang in the shop window
frosted white. Inside:
    fur collars, a mantle

brocaded into a private spring.
What news can you bring here?
    You never were

my sister. You cut my patterns
close after my own hand. The burr
    at the back of a copper plate

breaks the skin like this: everything
I do, you follow. Two pairs
    step where I go.

I make a yellow dress on New Year's
and you follow, one week late.

Don't trace my hand
along the silk you would never buy
    don't you ever dare

take this from my fingers, I am hungry
as a wolf just gone to pups in March
    and I will tear my teeth in bone

Knitting

When are you coming back to stand in front of the window?
(I heard you whistling last night. Cars pass me by all day,

waves circling the enormous globe.)
So much is left out, I'm knitting a pattern without

stitches, without needles, only long fingerbones
to carry yarn. There was something buried

the night I left Eau Claire for good, and I never knew
how it would grow. Now your childhood friends

are my students, I walk past houses you lived in
without my knowledge and your scent trails

from abandoned bakeries. Whole warehouses
have been invented to catalogue want like this.

I go on knitting night and day because I don't know
any other thing. All unknits by darkness

into twine birds use piece by piece. What secret
name can I call you? What adventure are you on tonight?

There is forgetting in the density of raw new wool,
yarn shop one block from your apartment,

the cheap scarf—you don't value things
because you never make them. Moon over the whitening world

sharpens spindle, windowframe. The sash
is pulled, seam is set: without material, there is no map.

Going There and Being Made to Go

Get back to the burnt-sugar basement, ceiling tiles
drifting like dogwood, the hanging rhododendron.
Neighbor's afghan waving granny squares from the couch.

Home, we've got roasting birds, the remnants
of potato, yoke, an open bed. Out there? Trinkets, trunks,
trappings. We've got stale cigarettes and stained sheets,

light from the cupola's circle window—glowing porthole, savior.
Ex-bedstead, ex-dollhouse, ex-rocking chair, you rose
out of this, resurrection and life. And open door.

Piano-heavy ancient brick. Frying pan and smoke alarm
distant as slumber. In old Ball jars melon rind and lemons
harbor years. Floor drain a lullaby holding the basement up.

Get back to heart-weed, jewel-flower, thorny magnolia,
arborvitae, bitter apple. Birthright, blossom. Nosy next-door,
clapboard, back porch. Swing it shut.

I have always loved to sit in ferry and railroad stations and watch the people, to walk on crowded streets, just walk along among the people, and see their faces, to be among people on street cars and trains and boats.

Ella Bloor

In the Wide World

All the parallel birches.

The night, where Orion hangs like a burn.
    Flaunting his six gems. Happy
    to consider everyone else from such a distance.

The students cramped in their desks.
    Their hands cramping around pencils.
        Lamp shades, eyeglasses, and library cards.

Hammer dulcimer and guitar, the viola, bass, cello, harp,
    piano, harpsichord, and all manner of woodwind.

        The babies waking up their sleepy parents,
        the scuff of slippers down a hall.
A Calder mobile, circles and ellipses and a bone in space;
seven fish swim the air above one child's head.

Eyes, deep holes, lakes, and ponds. People who drown and people
who do not drown; lovers, unborn children.

Roads that run longer than they run, interminable changes
in direction. And other things that are gone.

The owl's pellet made of bone and hair. The crow's beak
full of deer. Tendon waving in the dry wind.

Sharp stones and round stones. Cobbles, paving stones, bricks,
sand, and glass. Tar hot and pliable. Your twenty-six teeth.
        Urine and the smell of urine.

A man's cologne as he passes, arms in the air. The fabric
his shirt is made of. His loneliness—
                Lights in the distance.

And also streetlights, reading lamps, candles, and bassoons.
        Intensity and luminosity. Ohms, kilowatts, candlepowers,
        and calories. And stoplights and brake lights, all manner of red
        and glowing things, and rubies and garnets, drops of blood.

        Also reflections on silverware.

        Also lovers—

Things that are hard to forget all at once. Things that are hard
to forget piece by piece.
        All the bridges.

All kinds of musty and fetid smells—wet dog, stale air,
ammonia, a mother slapping her baby.

Waking up forgetful of a death.
                Eyebrows like moths in flight, bitter wine,
            orchids, and all sorts of softness: angora,
the inside of a woman,
            a homeless man's teeth—

Deep in the world are the windows, the insides of houses.
Rib cages, tempestuous, unnecessary spleen. The open heart.

Things that close. Doors. Scissors. Islands
      and countries, the line outside an empty store—
            Every ending.
            Every promise, eighteen wheels and ten tons of iron,
            freeway spinning behind. Everything forgotten.

The things you lost as a child.

Letter to the Astronaut

When the early stars come out into all that blue
it's like a prayer, one I memorized

without ever paying attention. I realize sometimes
that I am only waiting. The path of the satellite

eclipses me, so many hours removed from you.
And in the waiting, the sound of water moving.

What is gravity? Anything that could keep me
here, I can't refuse. So I find someone

who has the slender hands that you do,
hands I see everywhere. So I find someone

for when you are so far away from me, breathing
through tubes and doing rocket math, freeze-

drying your laundry. And I am like mulberry, he
is nightshade and by landing time

the branches are all tangled in vine. And then
you land, wearing all the darkness you could gather

out in the starred night. And I have to pretend
my heart has forgotten you.

If I ask you, do you look for me, across those light-years,
what then? I know your eyes don't catch

but break in shards of blue that splinter light
almost to whiteness near the edge, immersed

in radiation, deep buried. With what device
will you find me? This body is a faulty sextant

now, instrument no one uses. Our age of global
positioning, of cursors sweeping across the Arctic

Circle—you keep everything you know tied
in bundles of zeroes. And back here it is growing

dark, and humid the heat rises from the edge
of the street. Where I am

the chamomile comes to me dense and citrus.
And in a million years, when you find

notes in a ruined language circling
some black, collapsing star, I wonder

will you focus lenses to catch the light of this blue
place, will you remember how cut grass

overwhelms a lung in summer, how asphalt
burns from the ground up, what I mean is,

after so many flights and landings,
will you remember, will you come back?

Music for Landing Planes By

We drive Highway Q with no lights.

Millions of miles away, the stars
make visible energy, send it without expectation of return—
there's nothing like those circling constellations
for me, nothing but air rushing past the window.
Somewhere far from here, I can imagine remembering this night.

In your car, the radio
tunes half static. It doesn't matter to me
what gravity takes, only
the long, impermanent drop—
over the trees, we can see the planes come in.
They white out the stars: machines

for planets. *Lucevan le stelle* sings
the radio before you snap it off.
There is no other life.

When winter covers Wisconsin
there might be nothing else for miles but darkness
and the snow, and deer
bounding out of the ditch. So we go along
slowly. *Stop,* I say, and we open
the doors. Watch the storm front move out

and carry white with it, while the sky
west of us is clear and spins with stars. You
fall into the forgetful bedding
of the roadside—grasses and snow.

(The airplane's silver flash, the buildings exploding.
The bodies like sheets of paper.)

Late at night, early in the morning, I pray
for endings—at any moment
a satellite could lose its orbit. We are flying
machines we cannot land.
One night, I dream
of loving you; another, of falling
without ever coming to earth—the same dream.
Nothing changes except I begin to notice
bridges and high buildings, how beautiful they are
(how they shimmer like brides)—

Map of the Known World

I want to cancel her, girl tressed with grapeseed. Flax crown bowing.
Earthward. My hand could move. Something admits, lowing.

calyx corolla   anemone   anise   [beech, blue flag]

I have to hate her, arrayed.

Pine marten trembles fish from jaw. This is night in a jar.
Firmament. Not a diadem can own me. Oars.

And here, and here thin radiance: a deer's hoof severed
        and flattened, the red tendon.
The smell of loveliness. Great knot, little knot. Heron.

She has a daylily for a palm and there is no such thing as goodwill.
        Who says it is a liar.

(balsam belladonna   [slow rushes, the oriole, the bee eater])

Snow in a fountain. In her body are the bodies of birds,
(datura) [swallows] Am nothing, am only   [wingless]   sparrow—

The Bird Woman in the Dark

What   this my   left
      is my darkling
  my last   hour
Which & where
              ordained
     & lifted, water

(And the flagstones slick, and the little eddy in the gutter—and the
onetime hand on my waist, and the little elegy)

I remember I was somewhere in the gray afternoon with what rain
entering and piercing everywhere and under the bridges trains
would pass, roar
                  this is the static of my lost life—

What   has been left behind
What   have I broken being born
          into & between

(- - -, make me all syntactic beauty.)

& where & where & when,
& please   Sir, may I know—

Conversion

PS

In that kind of silence when there is snow
we kept walking across the bridge with its red rails

Maybe this is why the city shines
in darkness and the light drops away from the sky
on winter evenings: so that we can walk

together across an old arching bridge
and look at the white

and you can take my hand softly before you turn
back into the vanishing point away
there at the curve and say but maybe

tonight, maybe
and then in the quiet, the bells of a nearby church—

Santa Lucia

(I dreamt you)

(*I dreamt you were a little girl in a flannel nightgown shoveling snow*)

(I dreamt you were shoveling snow)

(You)

(I dreamt you were shoveling snow, the snow falling around you,
your white nightgown, your black hair)

On Hmong New Year a little girl waits on the train platform
in a pink pleated skirt with jingles

(I dream)

Crows have been flocking every night for a week to the trees nearby

there is still no sign of you

(I dream
    you)

You are passing just outside the window
Your black hair
        your white nightgown

Your dream

Finally the days lengthen, at first
such small increments I don't notice (north of here: candles)
In my dream you ride a horse by the window every night

Your black hair   the white snow

The white horse, the black horse

(I dreamt you)

(I dream   a white gown against white)
(The night rides closer to us

black on snow)

All Through the Night

(Sleep my child and)

The invisible subways of Washington, D.C., lumber on
Meanwhile my heart goes leaping across the continent
    stopping here and there—

All places unknown in darkness

Along an iron railing
marks on concrete the chimes of an approaching train

Turnstiles ticket counters gated grey

An peace atten thee
All through th night

What it means to wait after the last cars leave for Philadelphia
(after the midnight trains are gone)
I have been near cathedrals smaller than that

How marble wakes itself
How angels stand guard over dams
How at three in the morning the leak becomes a river
and how the levee finally breaks

Carried across a wire and in the distance a train still runs
the horizon smearing into dawn
(First birds' black silhouettes against the blue)

Amtrak, I will always remember you
sleeping huddled in plastic lobbies where Amish stand

And the look of stars just before the sky is too light to see them

I my watchful vigil keeping
all through the night

Your Love's Return

(Song for Stephen Foster)

Speaking of the miraculous illumination
    of the soul, I find I cannot
    go away from you.

In the cathedral, no waiting. I hurry
    past the guards. There are only fifteen
    minutes to kneel by the Pietà

to buy a postcard, to climb as many
    steps as I can. Even here in Rome
    you are. By the martyrs' tombs,

by the ruins: I see you.

Didn't you come with me long ago?
    When I told you I would fly
    eight hours to land, you stood on the wing
    of the plane and rode with me

and I was not afraid. The truth
    is you love me at my worst. In Manchester
    didn't you hang on to me in the spare bedroom?

Even when I don't think of you
    I think of you. Standing in line
    at the grocery store, walking Venice's

bridges: you. Next year again I am going
    somewhere: live in France.
    This time, like every time, I am sure
    it is too far. What are the chances

of finding you in churches
    there? A year is so long
    to be away. Meanwhile the blood

may slow. And here you will be guiding everything,
    numbers and names collected
    in your pocket, but all along speeding

next country to next country,
    nightward, to me.

Prayer

Let me live in Newfoundland
the town ratcheted tight October
to May   let me rest   this tongue   let it
approach new vowels with ease   Let

water flow black under ice   Every
sidewalk missing pieces
let me never trip

let me die in March be buried
in June   let digging claw break
teeth on soil   let everyone
wait let me smell
while living rich hundreds
of fish   bellies shimmering
sunrise by sunrise   Let me

scale ship's heart   be compass
rose for any man I choose   love
none live alone let me bring
pine oil turpentine   varnish
the deck with crack-crossed palms let

lips like holy palmers' hands dear
pilgrim   let this morning while ice
breaks deep in bay go on
and on let it   yes   let it

Notes

"Bedtime"
is for Katherine & Grace Seebeck.

"The World and the Ocean and the Sky"
Miserere nobis: have mercy on us.

"How My Name Came to America"
Go mbeannaí Dia thú: May God bless you; *Go ndeisí mé:* I will fix [it]

"And Will Be"
"As it was in the beginning, is now, and will be forever, amen."
"In the Beginning was the Word, and the Word was with God, and the Word was God. The Word was with God in the Beginning." *The Gospel of John, 1:1.*

Debts are owed to Philip Levine ("They Feed They Lion"), Mary Oliver ("Flare"), T.S. Eliot ("The Love Song of J. Alfred Prufrock"), Wallace Stevens ("Thirteen Ways of Looking at a Blackbird"), and Gerald Stern ("Lucky Life").

"The Way to Really Love It"
Salt ponds in the northeastern United States are dying off, a fact I first discovered via the links page on *makeready.org.*

"Matins, Standard Time"
Louise Glück's "Matins" poems can be found in her book *The Wild Iris.* ZCLC.

"Exclusion Pregnancy"
owes a titular debt to Carolyn Forché's poem "In the Exclusion Zones," from the book *Blue Hour.*

"Hail Mary"
is for Steph Johnson.

"Excavation"
is for Nicolas Collard.

"Forgetting in Multiple"
was written in Venice, Italy, with the aid of a Judd Fellowship from the University of Minnesota and an O'Rourke Travel Grant from the English Department there.

"St. Stephen's Day"
is December 26th, the day of the Wren Hunt.

"Dressmaker"
"Indeed, it is easier for a camel to go through the eye of a needle than for a rich man to enter the kingdom of God." The Gospel of Luke, 18:25

"Gnosis"
Meaning 'knowledge,' and often referring to heretical or noncanonical texts.

"Volans"
is the constellation *flying fish.* Written during Jim Calkin's horticulture lectures.

"Lejermål"
is an archaic Norwegian word for sex out of wedlock.

"Printmaking"
Etching and intaglio are processes by which a metal (in this case copper) plate is dissolved in acid and then printed by rubbing with ink and running through a press. Litho(graphy) and relief are other print processes. BA is the printmaker in every poem.

"In the Wide World"
was written on a Greyhound bus between Minneapolis, Minnesota, and Eau Claire, Wisconsin.

"Music for Landing Planes By"
Highway Q parallels I-94 for about forty miles, beginning at the Minnesota-Wisconsin border.

"Map of the Known World"
Julia Kasdorf has a poem by the same name in *Eve's Striptease.*

"Santa Lucia"
is for Laressa Dickey

"All Through the Night"
is a Welsh lullaby. Concrete angels keep watch over the Hoover Dam.

"Your Love's Return"
takes its title from the Gordon Lightfoot song "Your Love's Return (Song for Stephen Foster)."

"Prayer"
carries with it my many readings of Annie Proulx's *The Shipping News.*

Acknowledgments

I was lucky to have delicate and sharp criticism, guidance, and support on drafts of this manuscript from Laressa Dickey, Stephanie Johnson, Michael Medrano, Rachel Moritz, Francine Tolf, Shana Youngdahl, as well as from Bill Reichard and Maria Fitzgerald (both of whom always had or made time for my writing).

Jan Estep made my brain work harder every Friday morning. Peter Susag kept me in check on the girly stuff. Kirsten Jamsen called me her favorite living American poet way back when I was still writing things I won't admit to having written.

Michael Dennis Browne introduced me to a serious writing life with his special blend of enthusiasm and play, and I wouldn't have considered graduate school in writing without having taken his classes. Yuko Taniguchi's EngW 3104 was where I rediscovered poetry.

My students changed everything.

I listened to the music of Ben Folds and Josh Ritter and read books by Julia Kasdorf, Anne Carson, and Susan Stewart over and over while I worked on these poems.

Thanks for bribing me to memorize poetry from an early age, Dad and Mom.

Éireann Lorsung received her MFA in writing and her BAs in English and Japanese from the University of Minnesota. She studied printmaking and drawing at the Scuola Internazionale di Grafica in Venice, Italy, and she has taught high school in rural France. Her Web site, ohbara.com, features her handmade objects. She lives in Minneapolis.

MORE POETRY FROM MILKWEED EDITIONS

Blue Lash
James Armstrong

Turning Over the Earth
Ralph Black

Morning Earth:
Field Notes in Poetry
John Caddy

The Phoenix Gone,
The Terrace Empty
Marilyn Chin

Wu Wei
Tom Crawford

Invisible Horses
Patricia Goedicke

The Art of Writing:
Lu Chi's Wen Fu
Translated from the
Chinese by Sam Hamill

Playing the Black Piano
Bill Holm

The Dead Get By
with Everything
Bill Holm

Butterfly Effect
Harry Humes

Willow Room, Green Door:
New and Selected Poems
Deborah Keenan

Furia
Orlando Ricardo Menes

The Freedom of History
Jim Moore

The Porcelain Apes
of Moses Mendelssohn
Jean Nordhaus

Uncoded Woman
Anne-Marie Oomen

Firekeeper:
Selected Poems
Pattiann Rogers

For My Father,
Falling Asleep
at Saint Mary's
Hospital
Dennis Sampson

Atlas
Katrina Vandenberg

To order books or for more information, contact Milkweed at (800) 520-6455 or visit our Web site (www.milkweed.org).

MILKWEED ◖ EDITIONS

Founded in 1979, Milkweed Editions is one of the largest independent, nonprofit literary publishers in the United States. Milkweed publishes with the intention of making a humane impact on society, in the belief that good writing can transform the human heart and spirit. Within this mission, Milkweed publishes in four areas: fiction, nonfiction, poetry, and children's literature for middle-grade readers.

Join Us

Milkweed depends on the generosity of foundations and individuals like you, in addition to the sales of its books. In an increasingly consolidated and bottom-line-driven publishing world, your support allows us to select and publish books on the basis of their literary quality and the depth of their message. Please visit our Web site (www.milkweed.org) or contact us at (800) 520-6455 to learn more about our donor program.

MILKWEED EDITIONS EDITOR'S CIRCLE

Interior design by Percolator
Typeset in Mrs. Eaves by Percolator
Printed on acid-free Glatfelter paper
by Friesens Corporation.